THE ABC OF BUILDING WEALTH

GETTING STARTED WITH INVESTMENT

AMBER WILLIE

CONTENTS

INTRODUCTION

To achieve financial stability and growth in today's complicated financial world, a thorough understanding of investment is required. "The ABC of Building Wealth: Getting Started with Investment, equips the reader with the knowledge and skills they need to embark on a journey toward financial empowerment. The book covers a wide range of investing possibilities, including stocks, bonds, mutual funds, ETFs, real estate, and precious metals, and provides detailed information on each.

To begin, readers must develop a solid financial foundation, construct an emergency fund, manage high-interest debt, make a budget, and open investment accounts. Mastering investment research and analysis tools, as well as evaluating financial statements and market patterns, will lead to better-educated investment selections. Risk management and portfolio diversification are critical for long-term growth, and risk management measures are highlighted.

Value investing, growth investing, income investing, and dollar-cost averaging are among the investment strategies discussed. Tax issues are also addressed, allowing investors to optimize their tax strategy and maximize returns. It is critical to monitor and adapt investments, and frequent investment mistakes to avoid are highlighted.

Books, blogs, podcasts, investing courses, workshops, and financial specialists' guidance are all sources of continuing investment education. To demonstrate successful investment situations, case studies are offered. The book includes resources for continuing education as well as a dictionary of investment terms.

CHAPTER 1

Understanding the Concept of Investment

Investment is a crucial aspect of financial literacy and success. It involves allocating resources, particularly money, with the expectation of generating future value or returns. The strategic use of funds is employed to acquire assets that can appreciate over time, generate income, or both.

Investment differs from spending, as it focuses on setting aside a portion of current resources to secure greater financial well-being in the future. Instead of immediately consuming money on goods or services, investing involves putting that money to work for extended benefits.

Several key aspects should be considered when understanding investment. Firstly, risk and return are closely linked. Higher returns often come with higher risks. Different investment options offer varying levels of risk and potential rewards, so it's essential to strike a balance that aligns with your risk tolerance and financial goals.

Time horizon is another crucial aspect of investment. Investments are typically made with a specific timeframe in mind. Some investments aim for short-term gains, while others are intended to grow over the long term. Your time horizon influences the types of investments you choose and the strategies you employ.

Opportunity cost is an important concept in investment. When you invest in one option, you forgo the opportunity to use that money elsewhere. It is crucial to assess the potential benefits of an investment relative to other alternatives.

Diversification is a strategy to reduce risk in investment. By spreading your funds across different assets or asset classes, you aim to minimize the impact of poor performance in any single investment on your overall portfolio.

Inflation and purchasing power are also significant considerations. Inflation gradually increases the cost of goods and services over time, eroding the purchasing power of money. Investing allows you to outpace inflation and preserve the value of your wealth potentially.

Compound growth is a powerful concept in investing. It occurs when your investment returns generate additional returns over time. As your investment gains accumulate, the potential for exponential growth becomes increasingly significant.

Your investment decisions should be consistent with your financial objectives.

Whether you're saving for retirement, funding education, buying a home, or achieving other milestones, your investment strategy should be tailored to your specific objectives.

Understanding the concept of investment involves grasping these fundamental principles and concepts. It's about recognizing that your money has the potential to work for you, creating opportunities for financial growth and security. While investments come with risks, they also offer the potential for significant rewards that can impact your financial future. By building a strong foundation of investment knowledge, you can make informed decisions that align with your goals and aspirations.

Importance Of Investment For Financial Goals

By utilizing their resources to generate wealth, maintain purchasing power, and guarantee their future, investors play a crucial role in assisting people in reaching their financial goals. For financial objectives, investment is essential for the following reasons, among others:

Wealth Accumulation: Building wealth over time is one of the main goals of investing. You can create a sizeable financial portfolio that acts as a safety net and offers prospects for growth by wisely allocating your resources to investments with the potential to increase in value.

Beat Inflation: Over time, inflation reduces the value of money's purchasing power. Outpacing inflation through investments enables you to maintain your level of living and reach your financial goals by ensuring that your money holds its value in the face of growing costs.

Long-Term Goals: A lot of financial objectives, including saving for retirement, paying for a child's school, or purchasing a home, call for significant quantities of money that may be challenging to accumulate just through monthly income. Long-term goals are attainable because investments offer a way to amass the required funds over a prolonged time.

Produce Passive Income: Some investments, such as dividend-paying stocks, bonds, and rental properties, produce passive income regularly in the form of dividends, interest, or rental payments. Your primary income may be supplemented by this passive income, which will help you reach your financial objectives.

Risk management and diversification: A well-structured investment portfolio provides diversity by dispersing risk among several asset types. This protects your financial goals from excessive risk by balancing the impact of poor performance in one investment with profits from others.

Investments are crucial to creating a comfortable retirement nest fund, according to retirement planning. You can put money in retirement accounts like IRAs and 401(k)s with tax advantages, ensuring you have enough money to support your lifestyle after you stop working.

Financial Independence and Freedom: Investing opens the door to financial freedom. You don't have to rely exclusively on your income from your job to support your living expenditures if you have a well-managed investment portfolio.

Investments can increase in value over time, providing an opportunity for capital growth. As your investments increase in value, you have the chance to amass significant funds that can be reinvested or used to achieve financial objectives.

Achieve certain goals: Whether it's purchasing a home, paying for a child's education, or launching a business, investments can be targeted to fulfill certain financial goals. You will be in a better position to meet these milestones on schedule if your investments are coordinated with them.

Legacy Planning: You can leave your loved ones with a financial legacy by using investments. Investments can help with estate planning to make sure that your assets are allocated in the way you want them to be, protecting future generations.

using investments can help you reach your financial objectives methodically and smartly. They make it possible for people to increase their wealth, bring in money, control risk, and protect their financial future. You can work toward achieving your short- and long-term financial goals by comprehending the value of investing and developing a well-thought-out investment strategy.

Different Types Of Investments

Different forms of investments have varying degrees of risk, possible return, and liquidity. Diversifying your investing portfolio among several asset classes can assist you in achieving a balanced approach to wealth building and risk management. Here's a rundown of some of the most frequent forms of investments:

Stocks:

Stocks are ownership shares in a corporation. When you purchase stock, you become a shareholder and acquire a percentage of the company's assets and earnings. Stocks can provide significant profits over time, but they also have increased volatility and risk. They can provide both capital appreciation and dividend income and are traded on stock markets.

Bonds:

Debt instruments issued by governments, municipalities, or corporations are known as bonds. When you purchase a bond, you are effectively lending money to the issuer in exchange for periodic interest payments and the return of principal at maturity. Bonds are considered lower-risk investments than stocks because they give a more dependable income source, although they may deliver lesser returns.

Mutual Funds And Etfs (Exchange-Traded Funds):

Mutual funds and exchange-traded funds (ETFs) aggregate money from different individuals to invest in a diverse portfolio of stocks, bonds, and other assets. They provide built-in diversity, making them ideal for investors looking for exposure to a variety of securities without having to manage individual holdings. Mutual funds are traded after the trading day, but ETFs trade throughout the day like stocks.

Property investment:

Purchasing properties such as residential residences, commercial buildings, or land to earn rental income and/or capital appreciation is what real estate investing entails. Real estate can provide a consistent income stream, potential tax benefits, and an inflation hedge. However, it necessitates active care and may incur higher initial costs.

Precious metals and commodities:

Physical assets such as oil, gold, agricultural products, and metals are examples of commodities. Commodities can provide an inflation hedge and diversity, but they can also be volatile due to supply and demand dynamics. During uncertain economic times, precious metals such as gold and silver are frequently used as a store of value.

CDs (Certificates of Deposit):

CDs are time deposits made available by banks and credit unions. They have fixed terms and interest rates and are thought to be particularly low-risk investments. Their returns, however, are often smaller than those of other investing opportunities.

Money Market Accounts and Savings Accounts:

Banks offer these low-risk, high-liquidity investments. They provide a secure location for funds, but their returns are often lower than those of alternative investment options.

Retirement Plans:

Individual retirement accounts (IRAs) and 401(k)s provide tax advantages for saving for retirement. They can hold a variety of investments, such as equities, bonds, mutual funds, and exchange-traded funds (ETFs).

Cryptocurrencies:

Bitcoin and Ethereum are digital assets that employ cryptography to ensure secure transactions. They are notorious for their extreme volatility and speculative character, and they are not regulated in the same way that traditional investments are.

Alternative Investments and Collectibles:

Art, antiques, rare coins, and other goods that may be appreciated over time fall into this category. Their worth, however, might be subjective and determined by trends and demand.

Each investment has own unique combination of qualities, benefits, and hazards. Understanding your risk tolerance, financial goals, and time horizon is the key to successful investing, followed by creating a well-diversified portfolio that is tailored to your specific circumstances.

CHAPTER 2

Setting Financial Goals

Setting specific financial goals serves as a guidepost for your investment journey. These objectives serve as milestones on the path to financial success, allowing you to stay focused and make informed decisions. They can be divided into three categories: short-term, mid-term, and long-term.

Short-term goals:

Short-term objectives are those that you want to achieve within the next one to three years. These could include saving for a vacation, purchasing a new device, or putting money aside for an emergency. Because these objectives are approaching, you should prioritize assets with lower risk and easy access to capital.

Mid-term goals

have a time frame of 3 to 5 years. Buying a car, paying for a large house improvement, or sponsoring a child's education are some examples. These objectives provide a little more leeway in terms of investment options. While you may pursue slightly riskier options for potentially larger rewards, you must strike a balance between risk and accessibility.

Long-term Goals

Long-term goals are long-term aims that last 5 years or longer. This category includes retirement planning, purchasing a home, and accumulating large wealth. You can afford to take on greater risk in your financial portfolio if you have a longer time horizon. This implies you can look into investments with bigger potential returns, such as stocks or real estate.

Risk Tolerance Evaluation:

Understanding your risk tolerance is critical to developing an investment strategy. Risk tolerance refers to your willingness and ability to tolerate probable losses in exchange for higher rewards. It is a combination of your financial circumstances, investment objectives, and personal comfort level.

Consider the following scenarios: If the value of your investments fell dramatically in a short period of time, would you be comfortable staying invested or would you feel driven to sell? Examine your emotional reaction to market movements, as this can reveal information about your risk tolerance.

Lower-risk investments, such as bonds or money market funds, may be more suitable for conservative investors. Moderate risk-takers may choose a mix of stocks and bonds, whereas aggressive investors may favor stocks or other high-potential, high-volatility investments.

Matching Investments to Goals:

Creating a seamless connection between what you're investing in and what you want to achieve is the process of aligning investments with your ambitions. This necessitates a strategic approach:

Understand Your Investment Possibilities: Educate yourself on the many investment possibilities available to you. Different investments have varying risks and returns. Understand how they relate to your objectives and risk tolerance.

Match Time Horizons: Align each goal's timetable with the appropriate investment horizon. Longer-term goals can tolerate more volatility, whereas shorter-term objectives require more consistency.

Diversification decreases risk by spreading your investments across several asset groups. A diverse portfolio ensures that if one investment underperforms, the losses are covered by others.

Regular Review: Your financial goals change as you do. Review your assets regularly to verify they are still in line with your changing goals.

Keep in mind that investing is not a one-size-fits-all undertaking. It is about developing a strategy that is tailored to your own financial condition and goals. You set the stage for a more successful and enjoyable financial journey by establishing your goals, measuring your risk tolerance, and aligning investments accordingly.

CHAPTER 3

Basic Investment Principles

Compounding Power

Compounding is a financial superpower that may dramatically increase the growth of your investments over time. Compounding, at its foundation, is receiving returns not just on your initial investment but also on the cumulative earnings from past periods. In other words, your money begins to generate more money for you, and this cycle continues to increase over time.

As an example, suppose a $10,000 investment with a yearly return of 8%. You'd make $800 in interest in the first year. You'd receive 8% not only on your initial $10,000 but also on the $800 interest from the first year, for a total of $864 in the second year. This compounding effect continues to expand, and your investment can experience exponential growth over time.

The key to capitalizing on compounding is to begin investing early and consistently. The longer your money is allowed to accumulate, the greater its influence. Through the magic of compounding, even little investments can grow dramatically over time.

The Risk-Return Relationship:

The risk-return connection is a fundamental investing principle. It emphasizes the trade-off between an investment's potential returns and the level of risk you're ready to accept. In general, investments with larger potential returns have higher levels of risk, and lower-risk investments have lower potential profits.

Understanding your risk tolerance is critical in this situation. High-risk investments, such as stocks, can undergo huge price volatility but also provide significant long-term rewards. Low-risk investments, on the other hand, such as government bonds, provide more stability but may yield lower returns.

To limit risk, a balanced investment approach sometimes includes diversifying your portfolio. While higher-risk investments can be beneficial, it is critical to achieve a balance that is consistent with your financial goals and level of comfort.

Diversification: Risk Distribution:

Diversification is the technique of distributing your investments among several asset classes, industries, and geographic regions.

The idea is to lessen the impact of a single investment's bad performance on your whole portfolio. In other words, don't put everything you have in one basket.

Diversification reduces the risk associated with particular investments. For example, if you only invest in one business's shares, your entire investment may suffer if that company goes bankrupt. If your portfolio comprises stocks from several industries, bonds, and possibly real estate, the impact of a single underperforming asset is mitigated.

Diversification does not completely remove risk, but it does help you manage risk more efficiently. A well-diversified portfolio can help you ride out market changes and increase your chances of long-term development.

Liquidity: Achieving a Balance Between Accessibility and Returns:

The ability to turn an investment into cash rapidly without significantly influencing its market value is referred to as liquidity. Some investments, such as savings accounts, are very liquid, allowing you to withdraw funds at any time. Others, such as real estate or certain equities, may take longer to sell and convert to cash.

The capacity to find a balance between liquidity and returns is vital. More liquid investments provide you easier access to funds, which is useful for emergencies and short-term demands. However, these investments may provide lesser returns than less liquid, higher-risk alternatives.

Less liquid assets, on the other hand, may tie up your funds for extended periods of time but have the potential for bigger returns. The correct blend of liquid and less liquid investments is determined by your financial goals, risk tolerance, and anticipated needs.

Understanding and using these fundamental investment concepts can help you make informed decisions that are in line with your financial objectives and risk tolerance. You'll be more equipped to handle the complexity of the investment world if you use the power of compounding, manage the risk-return connection, diversify your portfolio, and balance liquidity.

CHAPTER 4

*Understanding Diverse
Investment Structures*

Investing is not an endeavor that fits all. There are numerous structures for investment available, each with its own set of characteristics and possible benefits. Stocks, which reflect ownership in a firm, are one of the most well-known financial forms. Let's get into the nitty gritty of stocks, such as how they work, how to analyze firms and stocks, and the role of stock exchanges.

STOCKS

An owner's stock, also known as their shares or equity, represents the ownership of the company. When you buy stock in a firm, you become a partial owner with a claim on the company's assets and earnings. Owning stock allows you to benefit from the company's growth and profitability.

Companies issue stock to raise funds for a variety of reasons, including expanding operations, launching new goods, and funding research and development. Investors purchase these stocks on stock markets, providing the company with the money it requires while also allowing investors to share in the company's success.

Dividends, which are a portion of the company's profits dispersed to shareholders, may be paid to you as a stockholder. Furthermore, the value of your stock can rise over time, allowing you to sell it at a profit if the price rises.

Evaluating Businesses and Stocks:

It is critical to assess both the company and the stock when investing in stocks. Consider the following essential factors:

Financial Performance: Evaluate the financial health of the company, including revenue growth, profitability, and debt levels. Perform a review of the income statement, balance sheet, cash flow statement, and other financial statements

Management and Leadership: Investigate the management team and leadership qualities of the organization. Competent leadership is critical to a company's success.

Take into account the company's competitive position within its industry. Is it distinguished by a distinct product, service, or market advantage?

Understanding the Trends and Dynamics of the Industry:

Understand the trends and dynamics of the industry in which the company operates. A corporation in a rising industry may have stronger growth potential.

Price-to-earnings (P/E) ratio and other relevant measures are used to determine whether the stock is trading at a reasonable price relative to its earnings.

Dividend History: If you want to know about dividends, look into the company's dividend history and payout rules.

Exchanges of Stocks:

Stock exchanges, which are venues where buyers and sellers gather to trade assets, are where stocks are purchased and sold. These exchanges provide transparency, liquidity, and a regulated trading environment. Two of the most familiar stock exchanges are the New York Stock Exchange (NYSE) and the Nasdaq Composite Index (NASDAQ).

Supply and demand determine stock prices. When more investors desire to purchase than sell a stock, the price rises. When more investors desire to sell than buy, the price usually falls. The stock market's continual movement is what generates investing possibilities and problems.

BOND

What Exactly Are Bonds?

Bonds are debt instruments issued by governments, municipalities, or enterprises to raise funds from investors. When you buy a bond, you're essentially lending money to the issuer in exchange for regular interest payments and the return of the principal amount when the bond matures. Bonds are considered lower-risk investments when compared to equities, making them an appealing option for investors seeking consistent income.

Assume a company needs funding to expand its operations. It can issue bonds to individual investors instead of borrowing from a bank. Each bond reflects a loan given to the corporation by an investor. In exchange, the corporation undertakes to pay the bondholder interest (coupon) at predetermined intervals and repay the principal amount when the bond matures.

Bond Types

There are several sorts of bonds, each with its own set of attributes and risk profile:

Government Bonds: These bonds, issued by national

governments, are among the safest investments. Treasury bonds are one example. The default risk is relatively modest, and they are frequently used as a benchmark for other bonds.

Municipal bonds: These bonds are issued by state or municipal governments to support public projects such as schools and highways. Municipal bond interest is normally tax-free at the federal level and may be tax-free at the state and local levels for citizens.

Corporate bonds are issued by corporations to raise finance. They have greater yields than government bonds but a somewhat higher default risk.

High-Yield Bonds (Junk Bonds): Issued by corporations with lower credit ratings, these bonds offer greater yields to compensate for the increased risk of default.

Convertible bonds: These bonds can be converted into a predetermined number of company shares at the discretion of the bondholder, allowing for capital appreciation.

Bond Risk and Return Evaluation

When evaluating bond investments, the two most important elements to consider are risks and potential returns:

Credit risk is the risk that the issuer may fail to make interest payments or refund the principal at maturity. Government bonds are generally regarded as having lesser credit risk, whereas corporate and high-yield bonds are regarded as having more credit risk.

Bond prices are inversely related to interest rates. Existing bond prices tend to fall when interest rates rise, and vice versa. Longer-term bonds are more vulnerable to this risk.

Yield to Maturity (YTM): The total return you can expect from a bond if you hold it to maturity. It takes into account the coupon rate, purchase price, and maturity date.

Consider a 10-year corporate bond with a $1,000 face value, a 5% coupon rate, and a current market price of $900. The annual interest payment (coupon) is $50 (5% of the loan amount of $1,000). If you keep the bond until maturity, you will be repaid $1,000. The YTM would comprise both interest payments and capital gains or losses resulting from the difference between the purchase price and the face value.

Finally, bonds are financial securities that allow investors to lend money to governments, municipalities, or corporations in exchange for regular interest payments and eventual principal repayment. Understanding the different types of bonds, assessing their risks and possible returns, and using real-world examples will help you make informed decisions when adding bonds into your investing portfolio.

Mutual Funds and Exchange-Traded Funds (ETFs)

Exchange-traded funds (ETFs) and Mutual fund investments

Mutual funds and exchange-traded funds (ETFs) are investment vehicles that allow investors to invest in a variety of securities in a convenient and diversified manner. These funds pool money from a variety of investors and use it to purchase a portfolio of stocks, bonds, or other assets. Mutual funds and ETFs both provide exposure to a diverse range of investments, but their structures and characteristics differ.

Mutual funds vs. exchange-traded funds

Investing in Mutual Funds:

Professional fund managers manage mutual funds on behalf of investors, making investment decisions.

They are priced at the end of the trading day's net asset value (NAV).

Fee structures for mutual funds can include sales loads (commissions) and expense ratios (annual management fees).

They are appropriate for investors who prefer to take a hands-off approach and are content with end-of-day pricing.

ETFs:

ETFs are index-based or passively managed funds that seek to replicate the performance of a specific index or asset class.

Throughout the trading day, they are traded like stocks, and their prices can fluctuate.

A mutual fund managed by an active manager usually has higher expense ratios than an ETF.

They offer greater flexibility for intraday trading and can be purchased and sold at market prices.

Advantages and disadvantages

Mutual Funds and ETFs Have Many Advantages:

Diversification: By holding a portfolio of different securities, mutual funds, and ETFs both provide instant diversification. This lessens the impact of a single investment's poor performance.

Professional Management: In the case of mutual funds, professional active management can potentially lead to optimized investment decisions. Passive management, in the case of ETFs, tracks the performance of a specific index.

ETFs offer intraday trading, which allows investors to buy and sell throughout the trading day. At the end of the trading day, mutual funds are traded.

Mutual Fund and ETF Risks:

Market Risk: Both funds are subject to market fluctuations, and no returns are guaranteed.

Management Risk: Active mutual funds rely on the decisions of fund managers, which may not always result in optimal performance. Passive ETFs seek to match the returns of the index, which may result in underperformance if the index performs poorly.

Expense Ratios: Expense ratios are fees that affect returns in both funds. Expense ratios that are too high can eat into your investment gains.

4.3.3 Selecting the Best Fund

Consider the following factors when deciding between mutual funds and ETFs:

Is your investment strategy active management (mutual funds) or passive management/index tracking (ETFs)?

Fees: Examine the expense ratios and any other costs associated with the fund.

Trading Style: Do you prefer intraday (ETFs) or end-of-day (mutual funds) trading?

Tax Efficiency: Because of their structure, ETFs are more tax-efficient.

Investment Objectives: Does the fund match your financial objectives and risk tolerance?

Assume you want to invest in the stock market while keeping your costs to a minimum. An ETF that tracks a broad stock market index (such as the S& P 500) may be a more cost-effective option due to its diversification and lower expenses.

To summarize, mutual funds and exchange-traded funds (ETFs) provide a diversified approach to investing, each with its own structure, benefits, and risks. You can make an informed decision about which fund type is best for your investment strategy by understanding the distinctions, comparing costs, and considering your investment goals.

Commercial Real Estate

Real estate is a tangible and potentially profitable investment option that entails purchasing properties in order to generate income and capital appreciation. It provides a wide range of investment opportunities and can be an important part of a well-rounded investment portfolio.

Real Estate Investment Possibilities

Real estate investment options include a wide range of properties and strategies:

Single-family homes, condos, townhouses, and multi-unit properties are examples of residential properties. Rental income is generated by renting out residential properties to tenants.

Office buildings, retail spaces, industrial warehouses, and hotels are examples of commercial real estate. These properties are frequently leased to businesses by investors, who earn rental income.

Investing in vacation homes or short-term rentals can provide both rental income and personal use.

Purchasing undeveloped land with the potential for future development can be a risky investment.

Real Estate Development: Developing properties from the ground up or renovating existing properties can yield significant returns, but it requires knowledge and capital.

Rentals Vs. Real Estate Investment Trusts (Reits)

Property Rentals

Investing in rental properties entails buying a home and leasing it to tenants.

Rental income provides a consistent source of cash flow, while property value can rise over time.

Hands-on management is required, including property maintenance, tenant management, and dealing with vacancies.

REITs (Real Estate Investment Trusts):

REITs are corporations that own, operate, or finance rental real estate.

They are traded like stocks on stock exchanges and provide an easy way to invest in real estate without owning physical properties.

REITs offer diversification, liquidity, and expert management.

They provide various types, such as equity REITs (which own and manage properties) and mortgage REITs (which lend on real estate).

Factors Influencing Real Estate Investing

Location: A property's location has a significant impact on its potential for appreciation and rental income. Properties in desirable neighborhoods with good amenities and infrastructure typically outperform.

Market Conditions: Real estate markets are cyclical in nature. Knowing whether the market is in a buyer's or seller's market can influence your investment decisions.

Cash Flow: When rental income exceeds expenses such as mortgage, taxes, and maintenance, there is positive cash flow. Negative cash flow may be sustainable if the value of the property rises significantly.

Financing: The cost and availability of financing are important considerations in real estate investment. Mortgage payments and overall investment returns can be affected by interest rates.

Property Management: For rental properties, effective property management is critical. Managing tenants, repairs, and maintenance can take a lot of time.

Assume you're looking for a residential rental property in a growing suburban area. The house costs $200,000, and your monthly expenses (mortgage, property taxes, insurance, and maintenance) are estimated to be $1,500. You anticipate renting it for $2,000 per month.

Rental income ($2,000) = cash flow - Monthly expenses ($1,500) = $500 in positive cash flow.

Appreciation: The property's value may rise over time, increasing your potential equity.

Real estate can be used to generate income as well as potential appreciation. Understanding location, market conditions, cash flow, financing, and property management is critical when investing in rental properties or REITs. You can make informed real estate investment decisions by carefully evaluating these factors and conducting extensive research.

Precious Metals And Commodities

Investing in commodities and precious metals is a one-of-a-kind way to diversify your investment portfolio while potentially hedging against inflation and economic uncertainty. Let's look at how commodities and precious metals can be used as investments.

Commodity Investing

Commodities are standardized interchangeable physical goods such as agricultural products (e.g., wheat, corn), energy resources (e.g., oil, natural gas), and metals (e.g., copper, aluminum). Investing in commodities entails trading futures contracts, options, or commodity-tracking exchange-traded funds (ETFs).

Advantages of Investing in Commodities:

Commodities often perform well during inflationary periods because their prices rise in tandem with the general price level.

Commodities have a low correlation with traditional financial assets such as stocks and bonds, making them useful for portfolio diversification.

Global Demand: Commodity demand is driven by global economic growth and development, providing exposure to various markets.

Commodity Investing Dangers:

Volatility: Because of supply and demand factors, geopolitical events, and weather conditions, commodity markets can be extremely volatile.

Commodities, unlike stocks and bonds, do not generate regular income in the form of dividends or interest payments.

Investing in Precious Metals

For centuries, precious metals such as gold, silver, platinum, and palladium have been used as stores of value. During times of economic uncertainty, they can serve as safe-haven assets and are frequently regarded as a form of "crisis insurance."

The Advantages of Investing in Precious Metals:

Precious metals have historically held their value during economic downturns and currency fluctuations.

Diversification: Precious metals, like commodities, can diversify a portfolio and reduce overall risk.

Limited Supply: Because precious metals are finite resources, supply constraints can contribute to price increases over time.

Risks of Precious Metal Investing:

Price Volatility: The price of precious metals can be extremely volatile, influenced by factors such as economic conditions, interest rates, and geopolitical events.

Income Generation: Precious metals, like other commodities, do not generate income in the form of interest or dividends.

Assume you decide to invest in a gold ETF. If the price of gold rises due to global economic uncertainty, your investment in the ETF will rise, potentially providing gains. If the price of gold falls, your investment will fall as well.

Investing in commodities and precious metals can help diversify and stabilize your investment portfolio. Commodities provide exposure to essential resources, whereas precious metals provide a safe haven. They should, however, be approached with caution and as part of a well-balanced investment strategy due to their volatility and lack of income generation.

CHAPTER 5

Getting Started with Investment

Establishing an Emergency Fund

It's a good idea to start saving for emergencies before you start investing. Consider this fund to be your financial safety net. It is money set aside for unforeseen events such as medical emergencies or job loss. Begin by putting aside enough money to cover 3 to 6 months of living expenses. This way, if unexpected costs arise, you won't have to dip into your investments.

Paying Off High-Interest Debt

When you want to invest, debt can be a heavy burden. Especially high-interest debts, such as credit card balances. Interest charges can quickly deplete your savings. Priority should be given to debt repayment. It's similar to losing weight before starting to run. Once you've paid off your high-interest debt, you'll have more financial freedom to invest without worrying about interest payments.

Developing an Investment Budget

Budgeting is similar to making a spending plan. It assists you in determining how much money you can invest comfortably. Begin by listing all of your income and expenses. Then look at what's left over. This remaining amount can be used as your investment budget. Remember that it's fine to start small. What matters is that you develop the habit of investing on a regular basis.

Establishing an Investment Account

You'll need a special account called an investment account to invest. It functions as a container for your investments. Individual brokerage accounts and retirement accounts (such as IRAs or 401(k)s) are two types of investment accounts. Choose the one that best fits your objectives. Opening an account requires some paperwork and personal information, but it is a necessary step before you can begin investing.

Creating an Investment Plan

An investment strategy is similar to a financial game plan. It is determined by your objectives and risk tolerance. Begin by considering your financial objectives. Are you planning to invest for retirement, a home, or something else? Then consider how at ease you are with risk. Some investments are riskier than others, but the rewards may be greater. Balance is essential. Your strategy will assist you in determining where to invest your money and how to manage it over time.

Why Is It Important?

This chapter is critical since it sets the tone for the rest of your investment journey. By establishing a firm financial foundation, paying off high-interest debt, forming a budget, opening an investing account, and devising a strategy, you can achieve long-term success.

Let me motivate you! Consider this chapter to be the starting line for a marathon. The preparations you make here will allow you to stay on track and attain your financial goal. It's all about creating a firm foundation so you can confidently begin your financial adventure.

CHAPTER 6

Investment Analysis and Research

For investors, investment research and analysis are akin to detective work. It is about researching information so that you can make informed decisions about where to invest your money. Let's take a look at the various research and analysis methods.

Fundamental Examination

Assume you want to buy a car. Fundamental analysis is analogous to inspecting the engine, mileage, and history of a car. Fundamental analysis examines a company's financial health, performance, and potential for growth. This includes examining its revenue, profits, debts, and other financial information. You want to know if the company is stable and likely to thrive in the long run. This method is especially useful for long-term investors who are interested in the underlying value of the company.

Technical Evaluation

Consider checking the car's speedometer and gauges. Looking at a company's stock chart to understand its price movements is an example of technical analysis. Patterns and trends in stock prices, trading volumes, and other market indicators are studied. This method assumes that past price movements can be used to forecast future trends. It is frequently used by short-term traders who are concerned with timing their buy and sell decisions.

Financial Statement Analysis

Financial statements function similarly to a company's report card. When you read financial statements, you are looking at the income statement, balance sheet, and cash flow statement of the company. These documents show how much money the company makes, what it owns and owes, and how cash flows in and out of the company. Reading financial statements can help you understand a company's financial position, how efficiently it is managed, and whether or not it is profitable.

Market Trend Analysis

Assume you're predicting the weather based on weather patterns. Analyzing market trends is similar. It entails researching broader economic and market trends that may have an impact on your investments. For example, if you notice that technology companies are thriving, you may decide to invest in stocks related to technology. Interest rates, consumer behavior, and geopolitical events can all have an impact on market trends.

CHAPTER 7

Risk Management and
Portfolio Diversification

Although investing can be thrilling, there are hazards involved. You should use caution and develop a strategy, just like when crossing the street. Risk management and portfolio diversification play a role in this. Let's simplify these ideas so that everybody may grasp them.

Knowledge of Risk Management

See risk management as fastening your seatbelt while driving. Protecting yourself is the goal. Risk management in investing refers to adopting measures to reduce the likelihood of suffering a significant financial loss. You achieve this by distributing your investments among various asset classes. The other investments can assist in restoring balance if one doesn't perform properly.

For example, suppose you had \$1,000 to invest. You may invest it as follows: \$500 in stocks, \$300 in bonds, and \$200 in real estate, as opposed to investing it all in one company's stock. In this manner, even if the stock value declines, your other investments may maintain or even increase in value.

Making a Diversified Portfolio

The concept of diversification is analogous to a basket of various fruits. It's important to spread your financial and emotional risks. When you build a diverse portfolio, you distribute your funds among various investment categories. Stocks, bonds, real estate, and other assets may be included. Every investment has unique risks and benefits. By diversifying, you can reduce the negative effects of a single investment's underperformance on your portfolio as a whole.

Consider your financial portfolio to be like a pizza, for instance. Instead of ordering a single-topping pizza, you order several slices with various toppings. In this manner, you can still enjoy the toppings even if you don't like them.

Rebalancing Your Portfolio

Rebalancing is similar to tuning your vehicle. If your investments increase at different rates over time, your portfolio may become imbalanced. Rebalancing involves making changes to your investments to get them back into the proper mix. This maintains alignment between your portfolio and your goals and risk tolerance.

for instance, if you invested 50% of your money in bonds and 50% in equities. Stocks eventually outperformed, and today they account for 70% of your assets. To achieve your desired 50/50 balance, rebalancing would entail selling some equities and purchasing more bonds.

CHAPTER 8

Investment Strategies

Investment plans serve as financial road maps. They offer advice on how to increase your money while taking your objectives and risk tolerance into account. Let's examine various investment tactics to learn how they operate.

Long-Term vs. Short-Term

Long-Term Planning

See it as planting a tree and following its development over time. A long-term investment strategy focuses on making long-term investments and frequently holding onto them for many years. With this strategy, you can possibly take advantage of compounding, where your money increases on top of previously earned profits, and you can weather market ups and downs.

The short-term plan

This is like taking fruit off a tree. A short-term plan entails taking swift action to seize fleeting chances. It might entail making quick purchases and sales of investments. It may be riskier and necessitate paying closer attention to changes in the market.

Value Investing

Investing in value is similar to finding a fantastic bargain. With this approach, you look for investments that appear to be discounted in relation to their true value. You search for stocks or other assets that are being sold for less than what you think they are actually worth. When their value inevitably rises, the idea is to acquire them cheaply and sell them expensively.

Growth Investing

Growth investing is similar to making a purchase in a young tree that will eventually become tall. Even though their current valuation may appear to be high, this strategy concentrates on businesses with significant room for growth. You put money into businesses that are anticipated to grow in terms of operations and earnings over time. It may come with more risks, but if the expansion happens, there could be significant rewards.

Investing in Income

Investing in income is similar to receiving consistent payments from a rental property. Using this approach, you search for investments that produce steady income. Stocks that pay dividends or interest-bearing bonds may fall under this category. The objective of investing is to provide consistent cash flow, which might be desirable to retirees or those looking for a steady income.

Average Dollar Cost

Comparable to purchasing food on sale is dollar-cost averaging. With this method, you consistently invest a set sum of money, regardless of the state of the market. You purchase fewer shares when the price is high and more shares when the price is low. Over time, this strategy assists in reducing the impact of market swings.

Case Study: You decide to invest $100 per month in a specific stock. You'll purchase fewer shares if the stock price is high that particular month. You'll purchase more shares if the price is low. This approach can eventually lessen the effect of market volatility on your investments.

CHAPTER 9

Tax implications

Taxes are a fact of life, and they affect investing as well. You may maximize your profits and keep more of your hard-earned money by being aware of how taxes affect your assets. Let's examine the various tax factors that affect investing.

Tax-Advantaged Accounts (IRAs and 401(k)s, for example)

Accounts with tax advantages are similar to unique savings containers. These accounts offer tax benefits while encouraging saving for retirement or other financial goals:

Traditional IRA: You may be able to deduct contributions you make to a Traditional Individual Retirement Account (IRA) from your taxes in the year you do so. Taxes are due on the withdrawals you make in retirement.

Contributions to a Roth IRA are not tax deductible, but qualifying withdrawals from one in retirement, including earnings, may be made tax-free.

A workplace retirement account is a 401(k). Pre-tax funds are frequently used to make contributions, which lowers your taxable income for the year. When you withdraw during retirement, taxes are due.

Similar to a Roth IRA, Roth 401(k) contributions are made after tax, but retirement withdrawals may be tax-free.

These accounts provide tax benefits, making them effective tools for long-term wealth growth.

Capital Gains Tax

A capital gains tax is similar to a tax on the profits from the sale of investments. Capital gains come in two flavors: short-term and long-term.

Short-Term Capital Gains: If you sell an investment you've owned for a year or less and make a profit, you'll be responsible for paying taxes at your standard income tax rate on that profit.

Long-Term Capital Gains: The profit is regarded as a long-term capital gain if you hold an investment for more than a year before selling it. Long-term gain tax rates are frequently lower than regular income tax rates.

Tax-Aware Investing Techniques

Finding the most traffic-free route to your destination is similar to tax-efficient investing. The goal is to reduce the tax burden on your investments. Here are a few tactics:

Buy and Hold: Long-term capital gains tax rates may be available to you if you hold investments for longer than a year.

Tax-Loss Harvesting: You can sell investments that have losses to offset gains and perhaps reduce your tax obligation.

Asset Location: You can lower your overall tax payment by holding investments that produce more taxes, such as bonds, in tax-advantaged accounts.

Index funds or exchange-traded funds: These investments frequently have lower turnover, which results in fewer taxable events and can be more tax-efficient.

Case study: You invest $1,000 in a stock, hold it for two years, and then sell it for $1,500. The $500 profit is seen as a long-term capital gain, so your usual income tax rate might not apply to it.

Finally, taxes have a big influence on your investment returns. You may maximize your assets and keep more of your earnings by using tax-advantaged accounts, comprehending capital gains taxes, and putting tax-efficient tactics into practice.

CHAPTER 10

*Monitoring and Adjusting
Your Investments*

It's not a "set it and forget it" situation once you've invested. You must periodically review and make adjustments to your assets, just like you would in a garden. Let's look at how to manage your portfolio carefully and make wise choices as we go.

Regularly Reviewing Your Portfolio

Consider making sure your plants are flourishing by monitoring their health. Examining the performance of your investments is part of routine portfolio reviews. It's important to check frequently to make sure your investments are in line with your objectives rather than daily. You might need to rebalance if certain assets are performing very well while others aren't in order to maintain your desired mix.

Making a Knowledgeable Investment Choice

Consider picking the appropriate route on a map. Before making any modifications, information must be gathered in order to make informed investment selections. It includes researching business news, economic statistics, and market trends. You should use knowledge, not simply emotions, to guide your selections while thinking about new investments or alterations to your current ones.

Adapting to Life Changes and Financial Goals

Changes in life are common, such as starting a family or relocating to a new place. You'll need to modify your investment strategy just as you would your plans in light of these changes. Your investments may also need to change if your objectives or risk tolerance change. As you get closer to retirement, this can entail changing your investments to be more conservative or making adjustments for new financial objectives.

Think about investing in technology firms a few years back. The equities have performed well. But you see that with more competition, the IT industry has become riskier. To limit risk, you can want to diversify into other industries and cut back on your exposure to technology equities.

Keeping up with your financial journey is the main goal of monitoring and modifying your assets. Effective portfolio management involves doing regular portfolio reviews, making informed choices, and adjusting to life changes. By doing this, you may maximize your investment efforts and stay on pace with your financial objectives.

CHAPTER 11

Typical Investment Errors to Avoid

Investing can be like driving at times. You must avoid specific errors in order to remain secure and go to your objective. Let's examine some typical investment blunders and how to avoid them.

Pursuing Popular Trends

Running after popular trends is similar to chasing after a dazzling object. It entails purchasing something simply because it is in demand right now. However, fashions can shift suddenly. This type of investing might be dangerous because what's popular today could not be so tomorrow. Instead, concentrate on long-term plans that align with your objectives.

Ignoring Charges and Costs

Consider investing similar to shopping. There are hidden fees occasionally, but you can also find excellent offers. Neglecting fees and expenses can reduce your profits. Make sure you are aware of the costs related to your investments, just like you would check the price tags on goods at a store. To keep more of your money, look for solutions with lower prices.

Ignoring Diversification

Consider simply eating one type of food each day. Sort of like ignoring diversification. It entails investing all of your funds in a single kind of investment. You're in trouble if that one thing doesn't work out. Spreading your money out will lower your risk. Having a variety of investments can help your portfolio stay healthy, much like eating a balanced meal does.

Letting Feelings Influence Decisions

Have you ever made a choice while feeling incredibly happy or incredibly sad? It's similar to letting feelings influence investment decisions. It could result in snap decisions that aren't wise in the long term. Consider facts and research instead. Before making any significant investment decisions, take a deep breath.

Case Study: A friend informs you that the stock of a new company is rising. The equivalent of purchasing a car without inspecting the engine is pursuing that stock without investigating its fundamentals. Instead, learn more about the business and think about how it fits into your broader investment strategy.

To sum up, focus on long-term objectives, be conscious of costs, diversify your investments, and base your decisions on facts rather than emotions to avoid these typical financial blunders. These safeguards can assist you in navigating the world of investing without encountering unneeded obstacles, just like safe driving on the road.

CHAPTER 12

*Continuing Your Education
in Investment*

Like any journey, investing has fresh things for you to learn and discover every step of the way. Continuing your knowledge in investing may be enlightening and empowering. Let's investigate many avenues for financing education and advancement.

Podcasts, books, and blogs

See books, blogs, and podcasts as knowledge vaults. They are similar to having knowledgeable guides share their knowledge with you. There are many materials available that describe investment techniques, success stories, and even typical errors to avoid. On your journey toward investing, staying informed and motivated can be achieved by reading books, following investment blogs, or listening to educational podcasts.

Workshops and Investment Courses

Imagine taking a course where you are taught by professionals in detail. Investment workshops and courses provide organized learning opportunities. They offer detailed information on a variety of investment concepts, techniques, and tools. These programs can aid in the development of a solid foundation and the empowerment to make wise decisions.

Getting Guidance from Financial Experts

Think about asking a local guide for directions in a new city when you seek financial professional help. Financial experts, such as financial consultants, can offer specialized advice based on your particular circumstances. They can assist you in making difficult financial decisions, creating a personalized investment plan, and setting reasonable goals.

Why is it Important

Investments are a dynamic industry. Market trends shift, fresh possibilities materialize, and tactics adapt. By continuing your education in investments, you give yourself the tools you need to adapt and make wise decisions. You may remain on top of trends by learning from professionals through books, classes, or financial advisors.

Imagine that you are a captain of a ship. You get more capable of navigating the investing waters as you learn new information. Knowing more enables you to make decisions that are in line with your financial objectives and gives you the confidence to do so. So, take advantage of the chance to study and develop in the field of investments. You can potentially do more on your investment path the more you understand.

CHAPTER 13

*Real-World Investment
Scenarios in Case Studies*

Imagine enjoying a cup of coffee while you listen to motivational accounts from actual people who used wise investing to attain their financial objectives. Similar to success tales, case studies can inspire and direct you on your own investment journey and this are basically from experience and research analysis carry out.

Case Study 1: The Stock Market Enthusiast

Sarah is a young professional who has just started her career and wants to invest in the stock market. She has some savings and is considering investing in individual stocks. She's interested in technology companies, particularly those in the electric vehicle (EV) sector. Sarah's case highlights the importance of conducting thorough research, diversifying her portfolio, and understanding the risks associated with investing in individual stocks.

Case Study 2: The Conservative Investor

John and Jane are a couple approaching retirement age. They want to invest their savings for income and capital preservation. They are risk-averse and want to minimize the chances of losing money. This case study explores the concept of conservative investing, emphasizing bonds, and dividend-paying stocks, and the role of financial advisors in tailoring an investment strategy to match their risk tolerance and goals.

Case Study 3: The Real Estate Investor

David is interested in real estate as an investment. He's considering buying a rental property in a growing urban area. This case study discusses the advantages and challenges of real estate investing, such as property selection, financing options, property management, and potential pitfalls.

Case Study 4: The Retirement Planner

Emily is a middle-aged professional who wants to plan for her retirement. She has a 401(k) through her employer and is unsure about how to allocate her investments to achieve her retirement goals. This case study focuses on retirement planning, including asset allocation, the importance of long-term investing, and the benefits of tax-advantaged accounts.

Case Study 5: The Entrepreneurial Investor

Michael has a successful tech startup and wants to diversify his investments. He's considering venture capital investments in early-stage startups. This case study delves into the world of venture capital, discussing the process of identifying promising startups, conducting due diligence, and managing the risks associated with this high-risk, high-reward form of investment.

These case studies showcase various investment scenarios, each with its unique objectives, risk profiles, and strategies. They can help newcomers to the world of investment gain a better understanding of the options available and the factors to consider when making investment decisions.

GLOSSARY

Definitions of Investment Terms

A distinct terminology specific to investing is used. It's helpful to comprehend important terminologies that are frequently employed in the financial industry in order to move confidently through it. The following glossary will help you understand these terms:

Asset allocation is the process of dividing up your money among various assets, such as stocks, bonds, and real estate, in order to balance risk and prospective returns.

A bear market is a time when stock values are falling, generally by 20% or more from recent highs and frequently accompanied by gloomy economic predictions.

A period of rising stock prices fueled by robust investor confidence and burgeoning the economy is known as a bull market.

Spreading your investments across several assets or industries in order to lower risk is known as diversification. just like you wouldn't put all your eggs in one basket.

A percentage of a company's profits that is given as a dividend to its shareholders; frequently paid on a regular basis in cash.

Exchange-Traded Fund (ETF): A sort of investment fund that provides exposure to a variety of assets and is traded on stock markets like a stock.

A type of mutual fund or ETF known as an index fund seeks to mimic the performance of a particular market index, such as the S&P 500.

Liquidity: The ease and speed with which an investment can be turned into cash without materially altering its value.

A company's market capitalization is determined by multiplying the share price by the number of outstanding shares to determine the total value of its outstanding stock.

Stocks, bonds, real estate, and other investments are included in your portfolio.

Return: The gain or loss a financial investment makes over a given time period, expressed as a percentage of the initial investment.

Your level of comfort with the potential ups and downs of investing is referred to as risk tolerance. Your investment decisions are influenced by it.

Stock: An ownership stake in a business that entitles you to a share of its assets and profits.

Volatility: The degree to which the value of an investment changes over time. Higher price swings are a sign of high volatility.

Yield: A measure of an investment's income that is frequently expressed as a percentage of the investment's cost.

What Makes It Important

Similar to learning the local language when traveling, understanding these investment words is essential. It gives you the power to speak clearly, make wise choices, and cut out misunderstandings

by speaking with others about investments with assurance since you are familiar with the terms. Understanding these words can help you become more financially literate and take charge of your future finances.

In conclusion, understanding these financial jargon will help you become a more confident investor. Understanding investment jargon opens doors to making better financial decisions, much as learning a language does.

www.ingramcontent.com/pod-product-compliance
Lightning Source LLC
Chambersburg PA
CBHW060840260726
48661CB00002B/512